BRITTON C

THE LEADERSHIP CODE

"A SIMPLE GUIDE TO AMPLIFYING YOUR

MINDSET AND METHODS"

BY

BRITTON COSTA

THE LEADERSHIP CODE

Ordering Information: Quantity sales. Special discounts are available on quantity purchases by corporations, associations, and others. Orders by U.S. trade bookstores and wholesalers. Please contact Britton Costa www.brittoncosta.com

DREAMSTARTERS

Edited and Marketed By DreamStarters University
www.DreamStartersUniversity.com

"People ask if you're working harder or if you're working smarter. For the Grustle, the answer is BOTH. It has to be both for an elite performer."

Britton Costa

Table of Contents

Run Your Race 6

Roots Create Your Fruits 17

Imagination Over Memory 25

Be a Student: Water Your Garden 33

Chase Purpose, Not Paper 43

Flawless Vision 51

Know Your Role: Mastering Every Position 58

All In: No Plan B 65

Grustle: Grind vs. Hustle 75

Be True to Who You Are: Authentic Swag 83

Goal Diggin'—Lead by Design Not By Default 90

Get R.I.C.H. -- Realize I Create Happiness 98

S.C.A.M. Your People 105

Unification of a Team 113

Mindset: Learn to Be Mentally Tough 122

This book is for the leader in all of us. I wanted to put everything that I have learned about leadership and how to create an unstoppable legacy into a simple guide for anyone to read. This includes lessons that I picked up on my own, and many facets that I have learned directly from others. Until recently, I didn't realize that I lived by a "code" in business. I was simply doing what I know what works best. Now, it's time to share that code with you.

Britton Costa

Chapter 1

Run Your Race

Throughout our lives, excuses will always be there, opportunity won't. This book will provide the guidance, experience, motivation and inspiration to instruct and encourage you to apply laser focus as you make life-changing leadership moves with proven results. Today is your day to begin in a new direction that will position you to achieve your true potential as a leader. The leadership lessons and experiences I will share with you will put the rubber to the road and will change your life, just as they have changed mine. But you have to want it. You have to commit to it.

My name is Britton Costa, just an average guy, who didn't quit. I felt a fire inside me to constantly learn, develop, improve and strengthen, so that I was never stagnant and always propelled forward and upward. I set goals, stayed true to myself, and stayed the course no matter the obstacles.

Now, I'd be lying if I said that it was an easy and perfect journey -- in truth, I have faced a lion's share of adversity along the way. The difference was that I chose not to quit, and instead maintained the wisdom and discipline to press on toward my path of purpose. I knew and fully believed, that when things got tough, *it meant that I was going to level up, not level off.* Sure, I could have quit, I could have made excuses or taken the victim mentality, but what sort of leader would I be? Who would want to follow someone that lacks control, persistence and confidence? Instead, I diligently continued my climb professionally while switching career fields, starting at the bottom all over again, and quickly worked my way to the top to a successful leadership role.

Today I have found success in the private sector as a Director of Talent Acquisition, Regional General Manager and a Sales Director. I am a public speaker and produce motivational content on social media through The G.R.I.N.D., so that I can fulfill my purpose of elevating others, like you.

If you're reading this book, odds are you feel that hunger, you feel that drive, and you know that the place you are in life is not the place you want to ultimately be. You are fully aware that there is something bigger and better for you if you are willing to put the work in. You might already be a strong leader who understands the value of personal development, or you may be fresh into your great race towards leadership and need some guiding lights along the way.

I'll be direct with you, here's what you're going to find in this book -- you will receive positive messages, results-oriented methods, inspiring quotes to internalize, effective acronyms, and honest (sometimes brutally honest) real-talk. I want to see you succeed just as much as you want it.

So let's begin this race.

If you're going to lead life on your terms, you're going to have to decide to make a *run* at some point. When I started out, I was misunderstood, people didn't see my vision, and when I tried to share it, they didn't want to hear it. You need to know that there will be times that nobody will understand, but your success is not dependent on their opinions and perceptions, its dependent on your *will* to fight for the life you want to live.

The fact is, some steps need to be taken alone initially. It's a vital part of where you want to go and who you need to become. Leadership isn't about being the exact same person as everyone at the job, on the team or in the race. It's about taking daily steps to be different and make drastic impacts in people's lives. The majority choose to drench water on their internal leadership flame rather than embracing it.

If you're anything like me, you don't love the idea of failure. People assume you're never supposed to fail but I'm here to tell you that's not the way of the world. If you fail or stumble in a previous race, your natural instinct will be to give up. You look at any great leader and know that they didn't get to where they are now by way of a straight line. They faced challenges, peaks and valleys, ups and downs, but they kept on the course. They recognized failure is part of any great leader's journey.

Here's another truth about your race -- you have to *start where you start*, even though you may not be starting where you ideally want. Don't allow yourself to get more focused on other people than on yourself, especially at the beginning. Everybody wants to focus on someone else's 20th mile instead of their own first mile. We have no idea the scars, which I label as "trophies," that these experienced and accomplished men and women have endured to get to where they are.

You need to have blinders on when you start your race and remember that it's imperative to stay in your lane. Look at the Derby horses, they don't care about the other horse's positioning or pace -- they have their blinders on and the horse just *goes full throttle*. They can't see the horse to their right, because if it slows up, they too will slow up. If it sees that the horse to its left injured itself, it's going to get paralyzed by fear and think of all the things that can't be accomplished, which causes the horse to overthink. The horse can only give it everything it has by continuing to keep its eye on the prize, the finish line, and not worry where anyone else is in their race. **When you're overthinking you're not overachieving!** Great things happen when you stay in control and stay in your lane as a leader.

The next thing I want you to know is that **the right action gains traction and momentum**. Running your race requires constant steps and movements forward to create *momentum* in leadership. One step after another creates the *momentum* of your race, which is built at the intersection of attitude and effort. Although I wasn't sure exactly what I should be doing at first, I always made sure I kept a positive attitude and gave maximum effort. We might have all the knowledge in the world, but we might not be moving. **Leadership isn't a *position*, it's an *action*.** We might be ready to start the race, but are we moving? If you are not moving forward, then realistically you are moving backwards. It's key that you *lead from the front* and *set the tone*.

I want to make it clear that there's a difference between *busyness* and *business*. There's somebody who says, "I put in 40 hours a week," but a lot of those hours are not spent really working -- there's no real action. They're procrastinating and coasting! Anyone making a championship run knows coasting won't win the crown. If you were to give 40 hours of straight action, you're going to be exhausted, just like that Derby horse that keeps going and powers through. How many hours are you willing to go full-throttle and push your limits?

When you go this hard and this fast, I want you to know that you're going to fall. But here is the great news -- you're going to fall forward because you're constantly moving. Action and momentum drive out negative thought and setbacks. We know leaders won't win by overthinking and never pulling the trigger. They know that it's never a sprint, it's always a marathon, and *action* and *momentum* become a true measure of success.

As a leader, if you're not getting results, the first thing I ask is "**WTF?!?!**" Yeah, I said it, "**What's the focus**?" Leaders aren't overworked, they just aren't focused on what's required! The greatest edge you can give yourself is focusing on exactly what you can control. So many people focus on situations that have zero relevance to their goals. In order to run your race like an effective leader, you must focus on your endpoint and not allow distractions to deter you from your goal.

Here is how I did it -- I call this the Triple Crown Focus. This system involves three tiers of focus: 1) Inner focus; 2) Outer focus; and 3) Other focus.

To understand true focus, let's break down these 3 tiers.

1) Inner focus is all about you. These are your personal goals, be them personal growth plans, fitness, health, educational, professional, spiritual, relationship or business goals.

2) Outer focus focuses on the growth of your team. As a leader you must find and learn new methods to innovate your team, your growth, and your ideas so your organization doesn't get stale. Having outer focus allows adaptability and flexibility to change with the times. Times change, environments change, economies change and of course people change. To sustain longevity, you need to focus on new ways to stay long-lasting.

3) Other focus is about uplifting and influencing the people you have the privilege to lead. This becomes natural and reflexive for successful leaders. It's one of the biggest components to their success and belief. The focus is on the team as individuals, while guiding them through a goal-driven road map and developing their speed.

Without all three focus tiers, you put massive limitations on your organization. Radio Shack and Blockbuster focused only on the inner focus, not on the outer focus of what we, as consumers wanted, and that is what lead them to shut down every store. They refused to adapt to the times and innovate accordingly. If you're solely inner driven, you will get blindsided with problems without people. If you just focus on yourself, you can't focus on anything else. If you focus only on your organization, you will not grow personally, and nothing will ever change. If you just focus on other people, and neglect yourself, they're going to catch you.

As a leader, when you're running in your own lane and going toward a goal, you must find proper balance within the tiers of your focus. When you master this balance, you now will be able to teach this mastery to your team. When there is no focus, the end destination becomes blurred for both you and your team, resulting in potentially getting off track. However, when the goal is relatable to the team and the focus is clear, it is very easy to stay on course.

If you have your team with you, you're going to succeed if you're all running towards the same goal. If you do see things you like from the outside, implement them into your own methods and evolve your brand and team. Stay focused, don't get distracted, take the best ideas with you, and apply them to your own organization as you keep moving toward your ultimate leadership goals.

There's a great photograph of a Derby horse who lost focus when he looked at the other horse and was beat by a nose! It's a game of inches. Likewise, in leadership, we're talking about inches of focus being the great advantage. Set your goal and don't look backwards.

As a leader, you're never complacent and cannot allow yourself to get stagnant. You must constantly pivot and make moves. I applaud you for taking the step toward self-development as a leader by reading my book. Are you ready to focus on solutions and accomplish your leadership goals? Let's run at them!

Leadership Challenge:

What do you hope to get out of this book? What will you do to eliminate distractions in your life so that you can focus on and achieve your goals?

_____

_____

_____

_____

_____

_____

_____

_____

_____

_____

_____

_____

_____

_____

_____

_____

_____

*"Stress comes from not taking action over something,
one can take control of it by taking action."*

Jeff Bezos

Chapter 2

Roots Create Your Fruits

There's the common question that is regularly asked and echoed, **_are leaders born or are leaders created_**? The answer is both! Obviously, they are born but also created through their journey which initially stems from their roots.

I encourage you to get back to your roots, to that starting point that each and every one of us has. I think for a lot of us, our upbringing and those core values in our youth are what bring us to the path that lead us to who we are and the leader we become. Unfortunately, a lot of times we get disconnected from those valuable beginnings.

As we get older and more mature, we forget the great lessons that were instilled in us when we were young. They say that we pick things up quickly at an early age, and if we apply those lessons from our role models, we will create our foundation for authenticity and success as an adult. When we realign and utilize these great resources it begins to unlock our second nature leadership qualities.

I'd like to share with you a little about my roots. I came from a broken family, not one of dysfunction, but of divorce, like many in today's times. My parents divorced when I was 10. Although it's not that uncommon in our generation, as a child, it put me into somewhat of a dark and challenging place. I felt that I was not "mantle material" – you know, the families who have pictures of their whole family smiling together on the mantle.

After the divorce, I moved in and was raised middle-class by my grandparents. In my grandparents' day, divorce was unheard of, so coming from a family that was broken, it created a unique situation that combined a modern upbringing with traditional core values. I'm talking about the old-school ways of raising a child that were common decades before I was born.

As a child, I looked at the situation as a burden, but it turned out to be one of my most rewarding blessings. To this day, I still think of the lessons and values that were instilled in me by my grandparents. Those intangible gifts you obtain early in life are not always revealed to us right away. The surprising blessings of this split marriage were more than just two sets of Christmases. Instead, I ended up with *even more* love, compassion, empathy and influence than I could have ever expected. I had all my grandparents, my mother, my father, and tremendous step parents to be thankful for that helped mold me throughout my youth.

My Italian grandmother is a pure soul, a salt-of-the-earth woman. She taught me to **ALWAYS do the right thing**, no matter the circumstance. She always had techniques in place to better my sister and me. For example, she wouldn't let us leave the house during the summer unless we first read for 30 minutes. At the time I thought, "You have to be kidding me!" I hated this routine like any kid who didn't want to read, yet she insisted. We'd put the timer on the oven and set it before we were able to go out and play with the other kids. She forced us to **do the hard things first**. One of her many lessons at the time that I saw no value in until later years.

Another leadership element I benefited from through my upbringing with my grandparents, was their encouragement of social interaction. They were always entertaining guests and people were always around because it brought joy into their lives. Being raised with these old-school values, my grandparents always encouraged me to have company over. So when I would get home from school, I would always lead the charge and call every kid in the neighborhood and invite them to come over to play some type of sport. It sounds little, but it was a big lesson on **bringing people and community together.**

My grandfather was retired by the time I moved in with them, but this man was a workhorse. He was always doing something, and never stopped until he was finished. There are people in **beast mode and others who are just beasts –** this man was a beast, no mode required. He came from nothing, so he gave everything, and more importantly, did it with humility. He would always remind and encourage me to, "Go to work." That's it, no excuses.

He was a man of strong will, who would never allow me to cop out. Through all his accomplishments as a silver star veteran of WWII and a prominent leader within U.S. Steel, he never found room to boast or brag. He lived by the motto **"If you're a homerun hitter, you don't have to tell anybody."** He embraced the hard work and a "no bullshit" mentality. For example, if you worked 10 hours, he'd ask "Why not 12?" If you'd work late, he'd ask, "Why not later?" Those were different times. That generation applied a true grind, never complaining or stopping until the job was complete. As disciplined as he was with his work, he had a much more humbling approach with the people he worked with and the family he loved.

Growing up in a multi-generational home, my father was also an integral part of my upbringing as well as the best friend I could have asked for. He was a man who believed in me long before I believed in myself. That genuine confidence he had in me forced me to have confidence in myself. He would **never allow my excuses to excuse me** from situations. If I would start complaining, be late to something or gripe about being tired, he'd say, "JUST YOU, you're the only one tired today. JUST YOU, you're the only one who didn't feel like going to work. JUST YOU, you're the only one who had issues today!" What he meant is that you are not the only one dealing with everyday life!

When you're young you give yourself empowerment assuming you have the world figured out. My father was quick to correct me on that. He would never correct me or embarrass me in public but would be very stern in private. At the time I didn't realize how much that technique would help me later in life, since this is a leadership technique I use to this day. Like the old adage goes, **"praise in public, criticize in private."**

When I reflect back on my roots and what was instilled in me, I have numerous takeaways that I apply to everyday leadership. From my grandmother it was to *always do the right thing* and from my grandfather it was that *there is no off switch* – **always finish what you start**. From my father it was always **believe and have confidence in yourself with no doubt** and **never to allow myself to be distracted by excuses.** To this day I still hear all of them in my ear.

As we grow older and more mature, we tend to shy away from the youthfulness and young-spirited methods that are helpful in leadership. As a leader, you never want to become stale, boring, dry and less ambitious. It is important to tap into your early roots when you weren't afraid of curiosity and adventure -- two great elements for leaders. Other important elements, from our roots, that help leaders if utilized properly are compassion, optimism, and belief. All of which will shine through for leaders in challenging times. It is also important to remember as a leader, to never take yourself too seriously and keep this youthfulness alive; not just today, but every day. Because in most cases that youthfulness in us, is the best version of us.

When people reiterate those lessons to you, it becomes imbedded into your DNA. No matter how much you grow as a leader, you will always hear that voice in your head, feel that instinct in your gut, and have the opportunity to make impacts with these attributes.

These lessons define me: **always do the right thing, do not give up until your job is done, and never accept excuses.** I embody these lessons taught by my family when I was young, and today I carry those with me every day in leadership.

Leadership Challenge:

What is the most valuable lesson you learned when you were young? Who is one person who defined your work ethic? What did they teach you and how do you apply that to your daily life/goals as an adult?

_____

_____

_____

_____

_____

_____

_____

_____

_____

_____

_____

_____

_____

_____

_____

_____

"Your brain finds happiness in mastering skills. It's been that way since you were little. So don't stop mastering life as you get older."

Tai Lopez

Chapter 3

Imagination Over Memory

When you are in a leadership role, it is important to give yourself permission to **hold big dreams and imagine the unimaginable**. Think back to when you played outside as a child. If you were a basketball fan, it wasn't *you* shooting hoops in your driveway, it was you imagining being your favorite athlete like Michael Jordan and the clock was running down from 3-2-1! In those moments, your imagination would visualize game winning shots.

As a young lady, if you weren't a sports fan, perhaps you envisioned emerald castles, yellow brick roads, and being the queen of your home with glitter flooding the bedroom floor. In those moments you were the queen of your world and couldn't be happier.

No matter your fantasy, dreams or imagination, you were mentally building something incredible, something with vision. **The leaders who are consistent with their imagination have endless potential.**

As we age, people start to tell us what we are, and what we aren't. Sadly, as a result, we get away from the gift of imagination. We may be told that we're not big enough, strong enough, smart enough, or pretty enough. When we hear these negative statements enough, we get away from our childhood imaginations and start living on the memories of what people told us. This is unfortunate because these are the memories of what they said we couldn't be, and what they said we couldn't achieve. These are the memories of their opinions on the goals we couldn't hit.

These perspectives and perceptions are shaped by the words of people who have *never accomplished any* of their dreams or imaginations! These words can pull us away and cause us to get distracted from our great purpose and our course in life.

In leadership especially, it is so important to be child-like, not childish. You never know, had you not gotten away from your true self, you might have been a great scientist finding ground-breaking cures, or you could have been a great athlete, but you got away from it because you were a late bloomer. Perhaps you could have been a teacher, shaping children's lives to make long- term impacts for a better future, but you were told that you weren't smart enough. Instead of embracing your imagination, you were thrust into "reality" by living off the memory that others planted in you.

The problem is that as we mature in life, we start to play it safe. We hang on to that negative memory of what they said we couldn't do, instead of what we want to do, which causes fear of failure. In most cases, the advice we get isn't from the doers or the dreamers, it's from the people who *aren't dreaming and aren't doing*. In all those scenarios they've already given up on whatever it was that they wanted to achieve. The sad truth is that **only 3% of people actively utilize their imagination** and if they do, it's often those memories and images of the fears of what they don't want.

Let's talk some truths about fear and failure. People are afraid to fail because they don't want fresh painful memories to add to those original ones. I want you to be reminded that all the great leaders have failed endless amounts of times. They learned from it, owned it, and in turn, ultimately grew from it. They fully understood their **imagination is one of their greatest gifts** and that anything can be built with it.

You must understand that failure can and will happen, however you have to be honest and open about it, stay true to yourself and stay your course. This is a key to growing in your journey. It's where you celebrate yourself the most and where you eventually see yourself. This will be the best version of you and it's where the dream starts. It's simply going into the future to bring your thoughts to the present. We all have to start somewhere. Why not start with believing in ourselves by turning those dreams into realities?

Believe in those great defining moments that are coming your direction. Every one of us recreates ourselves at some point in life, which allows us NOT to be creatively satisfied. You have to see what others do not see, while envisioning what you want to become. To become the best version of yourself, you have to hold onto those roots of youthfulness. Just because you get more mature doesn't mean you can't be *creative*, *imaginative* and *dream big*. **What is the point if there is no creating and dreaming big?**

Using our imagination has more benefits than just dreaming big. It also is a big component in helping with creative problem solving and outside the box thinking. A leader who uses their imagination often starts to realize it becomes the guiding light through the unfamiliar skies. In order to be the best leader for your people, you always want to use your imagination combined with collective action. The greatest achievers live creatively in their imagination, not in their memories.

Walt Disney is a prime example of dreaming big. Not only did he employ imagination, but he stayed true to his imagination even when no one else could see it. Walt shared this imagination and vision with many people who dismissed him. One in particular was a great friend of his named Art

Linkletter. Linkletter went all the way to the actual site where Walt Disney wanted to build the magic kingdom, hundreds of feet out in the middle of nowhere, only to regretfully tell him he was not interested. Linkletter stated, for every step back to his car from the actual building spot cost him a million dollars per step, which ended up being the biggest regret he ever lived with. The fact that Walt Disney stayed true to the course was not only magical but also showed imagination and passion that was second-to-none. He was the definition of a leader who perceived, conceived and believed in his imagination. His imagination ultimately led to his success.

Imagination is hands-down one of the most powerful forces in our mind. By using imagination over memory, it allows you to imagine who you want to become, where you want to be and what you want to do. ***Our big dreams and aspirations help us make the impossible possible.*** It is a gift to imagine what is possible far beyond what is predictable. Don't be like most who quit using this powerful gift of imagination after the age of 6 or 7. We all have an imagination, but few use it. Never let opinions, suggestions and research tell you what is possible.

One of the greatest statements of all time came from Muhamad Ali who said, ***"A man with no imagination has no wings."*** If you're going to soar, like the eagle, to new heights in leadership, you need imagination. Imagination is our gift to elevate us to a higher level.

As leaders we are created to create -- and if you're not doing it, then nothing great will ever be built.

Leadership Challenge:

Think back to your youth and to what you wanted to be and become. Have you accomplished those dreams?

If not, why?

What are your dreams and what will you do to actively pursue or incorporate them into your life?

_____

_____

_____

_____

_____

_____

_____

_____

_____

_____

_____

_____

_____

_____

_____

_____

_____

"Imagination is more important than knowledge.
Knowledge is limited; Imagination encircles the world."

Albert Einstein

Chapter 4

Be a Student: Water Your Garden

To become an elite leader, you must constantly grow. In this chapter I'm going to challenge you to take an oath for growth. Adding value to yourself is so important. ***Value in today's world, is the ultimate currency.*** The best leaders always know their worth but continue to add value. The second you stop learning is the second you start dying, and in order to be an effective leader and give back to your team, you need to become a lifelong learner. When you become a lifelong learner it cultivates a culture of learning for your team. Your main goal as their leader is to make everything and everyone around you grow, including yourself! As they say, **"You can't pour from an empty cup."**

I am a huge fan of personal development. I realize now that my leadership cannot play at a higher level until I do. Putting a high value on personal development goes back to what I shared earlier about my grandmother instilling the importance of reading 30 minutes a day, every day. Unfortunately, I got away from this practice for years and I had to restart as an adult. Now I am grateful to be surrounded by so many people who are into self-development, so once I started again, it became reflexive and second nature.

A story that comes to mind is about how I upgraded myself by reading privately which built confidence that I eventually displayed publicly. When I attended West Virginia University, I would beg professors to let me off the hook in public speaking class. The idea of public speaking made me very anxious. I would pace back and forth and unintentionally would drink a gallon of water to calm my nerves. The fact of the matter is, I was lacking confidence which led to panic. How many of you can relate?

One major defining moment with public speaking and with my YouTube videos, occurred on September 11, 2016. I was at a leadership gathering in New Jersey and you could see the lights shooting up from the Twin Towers Memorial in NYC. I remember I was hands-down one of the weakest links at this event and was surrounded by world-class-caliber leaders. Candidly, it was announced that we were all to go up to the stage and individually speak on any topic we selected.

I'm telling you, the air got real thin for me. I always liked to prepare, but in this moment, I felt very unprepared, no one had any clue how much I typically over-think. I was displaying my go-to characteristics of panic as I'm watching, one after the next go up on the stage. I then did some self-talk and told myself that *"I have no time to get ready, I just have to be ready!"*

I watched some others flake out and it was clear that not everyone would get a turn. I felt the pressure in the moment and said to myself, "This is a MISERABLE experience," but I knew I had to do it and found the *will* to push through. The only thing I could think of was to speak on the Midas touch and adversity because at the time that was exactly what I was dealing with in my life. When referring to the Midas Touch, I mean the people who went through fiery circumstances and used their struggles as tools to purify and grow, instead of permanent setbacks. These are the people who have endured a lot, yet still managed to turn turbulent situations into gold mines. Anyways, I ended up being one of the last two speakers of the evening, *and I conquered it.* I faced my fear, stepped out of my comfort zone, and it led to a bigger stage.

Two weeks later, I got a call from Eric Giglione, the founder of The Daily Locker Room, inviting me to participate in creating motivational videos on his YouTube channel. Eric is passionate about inspiring others and developed a daily video series with messages to help people live their best lives. This was a huge deal and a defining moment because The Daily Locker Room only invited a few people from the event to participate.

I then began to work with Simon Arias on videos for The G.R.I.N.D. (Get Ready It's A New Day). Simon has been an excellent mentor who expounds values of putting family first, but after that, is a leader, mentor, entrepreneur, philanthropist and motivational speaker. As a direct mentor, Simon is a lead-by-example individual. He focuses massively on his disciplines and has gotten me in the right frame of mind, body, and spirit, which I continue to improve on daily.

So, let's get back to that moment I faced on stage. The anxiety of public speaking diminished because I became confident in what I was speaking about due to personal testimony and *personal development*.

You know how you feel guilty when you constantly go to the gym and then miss a day? I feel that way when I don't work on personal growth. I believe it's important for leaders to always **find time to commit and practice self-development daily.** As a leader, you never stop learning. If I chose to stop, I'd let myself down and let down the people that I lead. I can't just teach them the same things over and over again, I owe it to myself and to them to constantly enrich them with value and a competitive edge.

Recently I was asked to speak at a seminar and chose to wake up early to read before it began. Any time I am asked to speak publicly, I read, because it helps to calm my mind. This discipline takes me back to my roots of reading personal development material. This exercise not only fuels my mind but helps me gain the courage and elite confidence to overcome one of my biggest fears -- public speaking. **It's important to put yourself in growth environments.** By educating yourself consistently it shows you are intelligent enough to recognize that there is always more to learn. If you laugh at self-development and education, you are only laughing at your growth and future. Always strive to become the best version of yourself to lead the best life for yourself. That constant input determines your consistent output!

It is a fact, in the society that we live in, everyone is so concerned about upgrading technology. You upgrade your iPhone, you upgrade to the newest flat screen, however all these material upgrades don't truly serve you if you don't also upgrade *yourself*. It is never too late to upgrade yourself. When we continually upgrade ourselves, we begin to reach our full potential.

Zig Ziglar talked about the importance of personal development in one of his famed speeches. He shared, "In my personal experience, listening to audiobooks every day for a year can give you the same level of training that someone would receive pursuing a bachelor's degree."

I tell people that you've got to make the M.V.I. (Most Valuable Investment) before you become the M.V.P. (Most Valuable Player). The six inches between our ears -- our brain -- is what matters most, and you have to water it with the right knowledge daily. *Only 5% of people in the world feel that self-development is the best investment. You read that right, just 5%!*

I truly believe that the most important investments you can make are through **books, audio books, seminars** and **quality mentorship.** The key word is QUALITY mentors, not mentors you wouldn't want to switch places with. Sometimes who you learn from is much more important than what you learn. **Simply put, I would not take constructive criticism from someone who has never constructed a thing.** You want those "walk the talk" type mentors whose results show.

I am fortunate to be surrounded by so many influential people who make self-development a focus. I find myself always taking notes because *note takers are money makers!* A lot of times people don't take advantage of stepping out of their comfort zone to talk to a person of this caliber, but you must understand, it's mandatory in order to master your own growth. The right mentors will get you to where you want to be faster, like they did for me.

I now exercise a discipline routine that includes mind, body and spirit. I read and listen to audio books during the day, I hit the gym four times a week, and to fuel my spirit, I read scripture.

In our office we do a lot of voluntary book reviews. Some of my personal favorites are *The Magic of Thinking Big* by David J. Schwartz, *How to Win Friends and Influence People* by Dale Carnegie, and *21 Irrefutable Laws of Leadership* and *Leadership Gold*, both by John C. Maxwell. But the one that completely changed my way of reading was *Relentless: From Good to Great to Unstoppable* by Tim Grover. It was very real, very raw, and I appreciated it. This particular book sparked and rejuvenated my enjoyment to read consistently again.

As a perfectionist and over-thinker, I have fallen into the trap in the past of not trying because I wasn't ready, or I would fail. I now know that the *more you are adding value and education to yourself, the more prepared you will always be.* Self-development is something done off the clock, it's your extra mile in leadership. It will prepare you to be ready at any given time.

People often say they want to be exactly where great leaders are, but they need recognize that the greats never stop educating and teaching themselves. By the time you get to where they currently are, realistically you'll just be where they've been. The best leaders always amplify their gifts and talents by being better than they were the day before. When you add all this skill, value, and education, it can NEVER be taken from you. By continuing to learn, you easily control your big gains in business and become the best leader you can be.

Leadership Code Challenge:

How do you practice self-development? How much time are you willing to dedicate to self-development a week? Are you taking care of yourself when it comes to nutrition, fitness, education, spiritual growth, and relationships? How can you improve in mind, body, and spirit?

Write down who your mentors are and how you can connect the knowledge of those who have experienced success to your self-development.

_____

_____

_____

_____

_____

_____

_____

_____

_____

_____

_____

_____

_____

_____

"Poor people have big TVs, rich people have big libraries."

Jim Rohn

Chapter 5

Chase Purpose, Not Paper

Many people read business, entrepreneurial and leadership books for one reason -- to make more money. I am about to blow your mind by saying this: It is not always about the mighty dollar. *For great leaders it's about putting the purpose over the paper.* It's your inner voice to why you do what you do. As a leader you want to connect and have a keen understanding of what your purpose is. A leader's purpose is what separates them from the rest of the pack

A lot of people do it for one of the 3 F's: **Family, Faith** or **Finances**. Sometimes their purpose to take on a job is simply for more money and to obtain the finer things in life. For others it is for their family, so that they can provide a better quality of life to the most important people in their lives. Or maybe it is for their faith, and to give back to their mission.

I am going to share a little about my journey and why as an effective leader, you need to find and *chase your purpose, not the paper.*

When I started with the financial services industry, it was because their mission, vision and purpose were so strong. This organization embodied the concept of serving those who serve and embraced many different outlets of purpose to be fulfilled. For example, we work with a lot of people such as firefighters, police, and those who built the roads of our society, just to name a few. I enjoy working with people and feel good about giving back to those who offer so much as a whole.

It wasn't until I experienced a defining moment in my personal life that I realized what this organization truly did. About six or seven months into my career, my father had a stroke. It was unexpected and, as a result, my mindset immediately shifted. This man dedicated his life to his family and my immediate thoughts were, "I'm going to have to dedicate everything back to him." It was non-negotiable. This unfortunate situation completely changed my perspective. Failure was no longer an option, and this permanently changed my current situation. Prior to this, I was going after more self-driven goals, but my gut and intuition told me that I hadn't yet found my purpose.

In my organization, we protect people's assets and livelihood if something like this happens to them, but I never really had a personal testimony. If my father couldn't do what was required, I recognized that now I would be required to help fill that void. The purpose became clear and when the purpose is strong the **HOW** becomes simple.

I can remember that moment brought on a landslide of both emotions and change. My passion with clients was totally different, my purpose in a team setting completely changed, and I started seeing change fast as I began to grow rapidly within the organization. Anytime you have a purpose it adds energy, drive and perseverance. If I was going 100% when I came in, I was going about 150% after my father's setback.

I can recall an opportunity to pick up extra work out of state. Without hesitation, I picked up and moved down to a place called Duck, West Virginia for six weeks. I committed to hotel living and a diet that consisted of coffee, Walmart sandwiches, and local diners. It was an area that not many were willing to go to at the time because it was in the middle of nowhere. I looked at this as an opportunity to do what others weren't willing to do in order to get the results that I needed to get. For weeks I increased my workload to the point of running on exhausted emotion. I was drained both physically and mentally.

This is where people get it twisted about moves like this. There's a difference between away **FROM** my family versus away **FOR** my family. I was away **FOR** my family so if needed or called upon, I would be able to provide for while my father was hospitalized.

This event brought with it a panic and things suddenly got real. I was no longer focused on the awards or achievement. Instead I was consumed by purpose, something much bigger than myself and everything else followed suit.

What a lot of people don't know is that I naturally have an introvert personality. Not so much because I always want to be alone, but more that I appreciate being at peace with myself and my surroundings. Around the people I am close to and trust, I'm actually the complete opposite and very extroverted.

This specific situation forced me to get out of my comfort zone and be an extrovert in all situations. I was suddenly pushing myself outside of my comfort zone because I had a "**why.**" A "**why**" is why you do what you do, it's your purpose. This situation gave me purpose. I carried an extra responsibility and extra weight, knowing that I had to do it for him. It was not just for me anymore. He was the bread winner of his home at the time, and by the grace of God, it all panned out. My dad is well now, made a full recovery, is more disciplined in his regiments and stronger than ever. This situation caused me to also become more disciplined and stronger in my own life. To me, he has always been bigger than life and now defines the definition of "what doesn't kill you only makes you stronger."

Once you find your passion and strength, you'll be great at whatever it is you do and enjoy it. It could be anything that triggers your purpose (like it did for me). Your purpose or passion can be whatever you're good at whether it's science, sports, medicine, sales, or people. *Every purpose has a leader and every leader has a purpose.* The leaders with clear purpose will always generate massive progression, even in the most challenging times. On the flipside, the leader with no purpose will never prevail in the easiest of times.

How do you find your purpose/passion? Many people do not find their true purpose until they discover how to align their strengths with passion. Although I'm somewhat of an introvert, I'm good with people because I genuinely care about people. This is a strength of mine and I have learned over time to play to that strength. People get so discouraged on their journey to their purpose because they focus on sharpening their weaknesses. Instead, if they focused on fine-tuning their strengths, their passion would not only grow, but they would discover their purpose sooner. Your gut will guide you along your journey as well. You will always feel those butterflies when you are about to do something great, something that's bigger than yourself, and catapults you to live up to your purpose.

Bernard Rappaport, who is the founder of the company I work for said, "You have to have a fire within before you light a fire in others." The purpose of a leader is servanthood. When you want to serve and impact the world, recognize that you have gifts and it's your responsibility to unwrap those gifts for the greater good. You can't stop every time you hit a mountain of adversity or an obstacle. **It's never a lack of skill, it's a lack of will** -- that's the problem.

You don't want to get stuck with 99% of the people who don't know what they want to do, where they want to be, or who they are supposed to become. Fulfilling your purpose isn't about what people suggest or tell you what you should be doing, it's following your heart and having a feeling of intuition from within. So often, if you don't take control and don't find your purpose, you'll have a couple bad days that could lead to a bad week, a bad month, a bad year, and ultimately, a bad lifetime.

It's about realizing progress in your purpose is much more valuable than the subjective concept of perfection. Once you find your purpose, your *will to win* is non-negotiable. A leader's purpose and flawless vision are the driving forces!

Leadership Code Challenge:

If money wasn't an object, what would you be doing with your life? Where would you be? Who would you be doing it with?

_____

_____

_____

_____

_____

_____

_____

_____

_____

_____

_____

_____

_____

_____

_____

_____

_____

_____

_____

"Success is doing what you want to do, when you want, where you want, with whom you want, as much as you want."

Tony Robbins

Chapter 6

Flawless Vision

There is a well-known scripture that reads, *"Without the vision, the people will perish."* The number one thing that leaders have to do in order to become great is cast a strong vision. The vision is the foundation to a leader's life. If delivered properly, it's a leader's best friend, like a diamond is a woman's best friend.

I recently got married to my wife. Honestly, I knew nothing about the 4 C's of diamonds -- there's color, cut, clarity and carat. People will give you their pearls of wisdom or gold nuggets of information, but the real key in leadership is to see long-term with a flawless vision. It's the real idea of what the future holds. All great visions start conceptual and in time, become practical.

And because I think you'll agree with this, I'm going to say it -- your **obsessions become your possessions**. This could be good or bad. If you focus on the negative, it becomes negative possessions. Likewise, when you focus on the positive, you'll be surrounded by the positive possessions.

Where will you go if you constantly focus optimistically on your vision? Mentally your mind will start to manifest these great things to happen. Vision is a 'we' thing, not a 'me' thing, when thinking like a leader! It's not about where *you* want to be individually, its more about the mission of your *team*, *company* and *organization*. It's about making a difference over a dollar and when delivered correctly, should encourage and inspire a team for success.

As I said a moment ago, vision is the diamond of leadership. The 4 C's of vision are incredibly simple and something I encourage people to learn and implement.

1) Clarity: Is it clear and concise? You've got to have *clarity* about your vision, you can't confuse people. In order to go from point A to point B, it needs to be simple and transparent. Everyone must be able to understand the leader's vision. It's very difficult for people to hit what they can't see. Clarity is the cornerstone to building your vision.

2) Compelling: Is your vision *compelling*? Is it exciting? Does it bring the butterflies? What's the difference between try and triumph? The OOMPH!! Does it bring the extra oomph to get people fired up? The most compelling visions are inspiring, never forced. Someone who is compelled has a fire within them. That fire burns brighter than any fires that may start around them. Someone who is compelled never worries about the *ifs*, and always focuses on the *how*.

3) **Commitment**: Are you all in? What you say and what you do has to be congruent. Your vision is what you stand for and fully believe in. When you talk commitment, it's *all in*. Committed leaders and teams stay the course when no one would blame them for quitting because long term it's about improving present conditions. Everybody hits breaking points, but commitment is the difference between the relationship that lasts 50 years and the relationship that lasts 5 years. When you are committed you don't look for ways out. The contingency plan is irrelevant for those fully committed to the vision.

4) **Community:** Does it involve everyone? Is it larger than one person could accomplish themselves? Leaders are creators and it's important to create a vision people can sense for themselves. This is the biggest part – it has to be big enough to include everyone's visions and dreams. Vision is very powerful, and people have to believe in it. If it's about one person's dream, no one will follow it because it's not about the community as a whole. Community is about

togetherness all the way through -- their needs, their desires and making a difference. **If it does not make a difference for everyone, ask yourself what difference does it make?**

Early in my career, my long-term vision was created to be closer to home and open an office. The vision was to have the opportunity to impact those who I was close to while having the opportunity to embrace those hometown roots again. It's special when you are dedicated to the vision and it comes to fruition.

Initially, when the vision is created, uncertainty is expected. However, the one thing that is certain is that there will be growing pains along the way. *As a leader you have to learn to weather storms* because you will see many storms in your life. You are either going into a storm, in a storm, or coming out of a storm, which is all part of the process when working towards your vision. Unfortunately, none of us are capable of controlling the storms. So rather, focus on the vision with patience and determination. It is important to live the quote, **"Hold the vision, trust the process."**

In 2015, the only thing that pulled me through the trying times within my organization was the vision we were all dedicated to. I was going through adversities, turnover, and lost some great people due to unfortunate circumstances. This particular storm lived up to the cliché line "when it rains it pours." The elevator started to slip and was starting to drift in the opposite direction. You must have a different type of tenacity when your vision is being tested. For me personally, if I didn't buy into the vision, I was going to break. As a leader you cannot waiver. It is okay to let yourself down, but it is never okay to let the people down that you have the privilege to lead. The vision not only defined the direction we went as a team but was powerful enough to get us to the finish line and through the breaking point of adversity.

If your vision is strong enough and you stay true to those four C's, it is the end-all-be-all to success. You will believe in yourself, your team, and any setback is simply a dip in the road. Vision is an essential piece to being a leader. You're going to have a lot of losses and how you handle those relates 100% to how you perceive your vision. When people look for keys to success, it's always multiple combinations, but purpose and vision sit at the top. **All great vision is pursued by great purpose.**

When one has vision, purpose and goals, there is little time for anything else until the mission is fulfilled. It is the ability to see the invisible before its visible. Your vision cultivates your culture, sets expectations, brings those big dreams to reality, and brings projects to life. It's the driving force behind all great leadership. Look within yourself, your teammates, and your organization, to set yourself up for a flawless vision.

Leadership Code Challenge:

What does vision mean to you? When looking at your professional and personal life, how can you establish a vision for your future direction? What values does your vision embody? Does the vision for your team include everyone?

_____

_____

_____

_____

_____

_____

_____

_____

_____

_____

_____

_____

_____

_____

_____

_____

_____

_____

_____

"A leader has a vision and conviction that a dream can be achieved. He inspires the power and energy to get it done."

Ralph Lauren

Chapter 7

Know Your Role: Mastering Every Position

If I stood in an auditorium before an audience of 100 people and asked them who wanted to be a leader, I can almost guarantee that 99 out of 100 people would raise their hand. But here's the fact, many of these folks never took on any sort of leadership responsibility and don't know how to efficiently lead.

When you see someone in a position of title and power, a sense of envy can occur subconsciously. However, the problem many will face is that they never saw this person's struggles before their success. It's not unusual to look for instant gratification, to start on top, but we all know that isn't how it works. When you are willing to keep an open mind, positive attitude, and master your current position, that's when you earn your way up. Not only to get you to the top, but it will help maintain and sustain that ideal position.

A great quote often echoed is **"Experience would be great if we didn't have to go through the experience."** When you take on responsibility in *whatever* role you're in, it all adds up, even if the experience isn't always positive. Take a non-business example, think back to when you broke up with your first ex, the person you believed was "the one." You couldn't eat, had zero motivation, and the only time you had peace of mind was when you finally fell asleep to then wake up the next day with that pitted feeling in your stomach. We have all been there, we can all relate. That experience came with lessons, humility, strength and direction for the future. You learned from it. Even if you did something wrong that led to the downfall of that relationship, you took full ownership and grew from it.

Whenever people understand the importance of taking ownership in their role, then more opportunities will come their way. People want to start with the monument, but do not realize how many hours it took to build. *It's those small millimeters that lead to the monumental moments in life*.

When you know your role and take whatever position is available -- it doesn't matter if you are cutting grass, doing dishes, washing cars -- if you are good at it, you'll eventually get the leadership role you want, which in turn will lead to more opportunities.

The process is never squeaky clean, and more often than not **shit will happen so shift can happen for you**. My testimony started in an entirely different industry than I am in now. I was in a successful steel industry for years earning multiple six figures until the recession hit our economy and times changed. The industry was a mess but what I didn't realize was that everything wasn't happening **TO** me, it was happening **FOR** me. It was then that I realized that the financial industry was stabilized. I watched one of my best friends, who was in the financial service industry, continue to thrive in those challenging times and decided that I needed to make a move. I left my career and started over.

I was hit with one of life's reality checks; going from thriving and being at the top in one industry to starting at the bottom all over again in a new industry. Like most of us, I thought I should already be at the top. At the time, I didn't realize how rewarding this "reality check" would be.

I knew that if I wanted to be the best, I had to be a master in every position. I knew that in order to master this new industry, I had to pay the price and master all roles and assignments that came my direction. Knowing it wasn't worth asking for more, but instead giving more to get to the positions that appealed to me.

At the organization I am a part of, it is an honor just to start at the bottom. I walked into the organization at 29 years old, and the only guarantee I had was my monthly bills. I was taking the risk to gain the reward. Fully aware that **"if a company is going to put a floor under your feet, they are going to definitely put ceiling over your head."** I was taking on a ton of new responsibility and embracing the opportunity to do more while gaining the experience at every level. There would be no floor or guarantees, but better yet, no ceiling which meant endless potential! When you own your current role or position, you never will be a victim. No matter how good or bad, there is always wisdom in those experiences and our experiences are by far our greatest lessons.

Before you know it, you're leading the charge and the experience you have acquired leads to a great deal of respect. When you see someone get to a position because they were handed it undeservingly, they can't hold onto it because they do not have transferable value. Transferable value refers to taking skills and values from past experiences, that can be applied to any field. They never learned this value because they never earned their value. Everyone wants more but you must ultimately give more to last long-term. You cover all ground when you truly know, value, and master *your role*. This is your blueprint to success. It brings out the best in leaders when they start from having nothing, to then earning everything by mastering trials and exceeding expectations.

If more individuals maximized their roles, felt pride, and took ownership, they would be more sustainable in everything that they did. On top of that, they'd be more appreciative and would have that *sustainability* necessary for success.

I want to remind you of this: **Your current situation is never your final destination**. When people are not in management positions, they often think, "Nobody is giving me responsibility," so they don't fulfil their role, don't take their position seriously, and don't demonstrate leadership. If you switch your mind to think and act for the position you *want*, rather than think and act for the position you *have*, leadership opportunities *will come to you*. In these times, it's not enough to just want, wish, and hope. You have to be willing to grab the bull by the horns and give more!

I knew in order to become a great leader, I had to learn how to properly demonstrate and execute every position with action. **Leaders make mistakes when they grade themselves by their intentions instead of their actions**. It takes demonstration and action, more than just talking and intention. Realize that your time in each position is precious and requires action. It should never be about what you can't do and always about what you can do at each position. When you begin to utilize your time and learn the things that matter, you'll see great opportunities open up and come your way.

Leadership Code Challenge:

Actions speak louder than words. What can you do in your current position to launch you to where you want to be? What can you sacrifice? What action steps can you commit to taking? In which areas can you go the extra mile?

_____

_____

_____

_____

_____

_____

_____

_____

_____

_____

_____

_____

_____

_____

_____

_____

_____

_____

_____

"I am not in competition with anybody but myself. My goal is to improve myself continuously."

Bill Gates

Chapter 8

All In: No Plan B

I just told you about the biggest move of my life, and it meant going from the top straight to the bottom. This move took a complete commitment. When I went all in, *I was fully committed to the commitment*. There was no wavering; I was in 100%. I knew there would be a tremendous amount of challenge in anything I did that was great, and was ready to charge at my goals without looking back.

As was to be expected, ***I knew that there would be a number of setbacks on the road to my comeback***. I could not sit back and rely on authority, power, entitlement and past success. I was going in as a rookie with nothing figured out. It was challenging having to re-learn and adjust. I walked into the office, I didn't know anything, or anyone, what I was supposed to do, or even where I was supposed to be. I couldn't public speak, I didn't know the business, and my suits didn't fit properly because I rarely wore them. To be completely honest, it was an embarrassment to say the least. All I knew to do was to give everything I had and commit to the process.

When you find yourself in a situation like this, it's time to see what you've got and discover what you are truly made of. You don't have time to continue to give yourself excuses on *why you aren't* going to make it, you need to fully commit and execute as to *why you are* going to make it.

I was my own leader, not leading anyone but myself! My first order of business that I told myself when I committed to this decision was there would be "No F's given." No, these aren't the F's you are thinking. Instead, it was F for **Friday**. I told myself that I'm going to have to sacrifice Friday nights, even though I was used to going out every Friday night with friends. The second F was for **Forty-hour weeks**. I no longer had the luxury of 40-hour workweeks. The sooner you learn that working 40 hours a week pays the bills and everything after is investing in your future, the sooner you will get to where you want to be.

For me personally, this entire adjustment was tailored to my long-term future. What I put in was going to be the biggest investment I would make in my life. I continued to have a tremendous *will to win*. When I started, all I wanted to do was win. I yearned for the significance of winning.

Some do it for money or awards, many do it for stability, others to be a part of a team and contribute. I knew I couldn't make a first impression twice, so I went out there and gave everything I could to win. I mastered the entry level role and was quickly in leadership, winning at a high level, and leading a team shortly after that. I put in the extra work that 99% of people don't do, because I wanted to be in the top 1% of the peers I looked up to. I left it all on the field with zero hesitation and I never had any regret giving my all. My mentality was so bought in, that every day I would find ways to win and improve at something. Whether it be waking up 15 minutes earlier, giving one more presentation, making one more call, or closing one more deal. My immediate goal was to obtain 5 little wins a day and I was committed to those wins.

Here's a simple analogy and the difference between commitment and contribution. *If you have a plate of eggs and a plate of bacon for breakfast, you obviously have a chicken and a pig. The pig made the ultimate sacrifice and* **commitment** *for the bacon, while the chicken simply made a* **contribution** *for the eggs.* I'm not saying you have to die for leadership, but let's acknowledge that there is a difference between a contribution and an all-in commitment allowing no excuses. This is how you know when you aren't letting yourself off the hook as a leader. ***That's the difference between people who commit and people who contribute.***

Throughout my leadership journey, I have come across some people who have more Plan B's than the alphabet has letters. As soon as you permit fallback options and are indecisive, you have already failed. My question is this... if the Plan B is so great, why isn't it called Plan A? It is easy to assume "the grass is greener on the other side." Always be careful how you conceptualize the grass being greener. This implies you will be in a much better position if you were on that grass or in a different situation. There are three things to recognize before you make that uncertain leap onto the other side.

First of all, no matter what, you are going to have to plant new seeds which ultimately means starting over. New teams, new systems, new missions and a new foundation to develop. Other times, it may be the opportunity that in theory, looks very plush and green from a distance. In reality it's actually artificial turf, and what you thought was going to be, never really was. It looked good, but when you got there, you realized it is nothing that you expected and very misleading.

Lastly, it's fertilized with bullshit. Excuse my language, but I've seen a lot of good people fall for this one. What they were being told and led to believe wasn't actually factual, leaving them in a worse position than they originally were in. They don't show you the entire picture. If you want green grass, take care of the opportunity you are a part of. Recognize adversity will certainly come and that adversity is the fertilizer to grow into the best version of yourself. *People don't fail from lack of opportunity, they fail because they have a difficult time committing to an opportunity.*

I knew I had to raise my lid in leadership and more importantly, knew what I had to do. This was the grind and I had to grind it out to gain experience. I was old enough and smart enough not to tell people how much work I was putting in. The all-in approach can worry people. I didn't even tell my friends and family. It's good to have people to lean on, especially those close to you, but they will give protective and mediocre advice. A parent's natural instinct is to nurture you and protect you, rather than equipping you to fight for what can be conceived as unrealistic ambitions.

Understand you're always going to be a **contender before you're a champion** and it's *inevitable* that your going to take a few hits along the way. This shouldn't ever be a reason to doubt yourself. The champions are the ones who never quit. As Mike Tyson said, "Everyone has a plan until they get punched in the mouth." It's a fact that the best take hits. I never told my family of my adversities because they would give the protective advice I'm warning you about. They love me and wouldn't want to see me struggle. The great leaders take those hits and use that pain to become better than ever before. That is how you create your greatest leaders.

My social circle didn't know what I was doing or going through. I was actually brought into the agency by my best friend, and then from that day, I immediately realigned my decisions and lifestyle. All the social activities, club scenes, and leisure time had to take a back seat. I was committed to making the sacrifices required. It was non-negotiable, and the decision was made to dive in with NO PLAN B.

If you have a Plan B now, you will continue to have a Plan B, making it very difficult to commit. If you take away the security net and make a commitment, there's no looking back. I can ensure you it's the scariest thing you're going to do, but it will be the most rewarding thing you do at the same time.

If you take any mammal and put them in a corner, they're going to fight. When taking a risk to change your life for the better, you're putting yourself in that corner. *You will fight, you will stare into the eyes of the things that make you uncomfortable, and you will finish what you started. With full understanding that the world doesn't owe you anything, rather you owe it to yourself to finish what you started and walk into your destiny.*

In the financial industry as a whole, the percentage of those who start and eventually quit can be relatively high. In our organization, that is not the case because of strong leadership. As John C. Maxwell says, **"People don't care how much you know until they know how much you care."** Selfless people in leadership roles care about people.

70

The number one product of every leader is people and we have to do the best to demonstrate that we care. You have to understand that the company does not make the people, but rather, the people make the company. When you put a high value on people, it's easier to build relationships and add influence. When both relationships and influence are very good it becomes easier for everyone to be **ALL-IN**!

When I walked into this organization, it was on the ups. You might play for a good baseball team, but do you play for a Yankee-caliber team in your industry? I wanted to play for the Yankee-caliber team. When people fell off, I knew that they didn't have the same appreciation or buy-in to perform at an elite level. Of course, they had multiple Plan B's. For those who remained, who were all in, I watched as they continued to grow. They became world-class leaders and that is extremely special to be a part of.

In the steel industry I flew solo. It was an entirely different setting. It was more of an independent approach than a team environment. As an individual, you earn trophies, not pennants. There's nobody to embrace, no unification, and no one to celebrate with. For me, *I wanted to be somewhere where I could continue to become the best leader I could be*. I loved the challenge and looked forward to taking my life and leadership skills to a whole new level.

Previously in my journey, it was just paper over purpose when I was by myself. I came to the realization of what was holding me back -- I was still holding back. It was time to go ALL-IN and STAY IN! Now that I found a purpose and had a shared vision with a stellar team, I knew that there was nowhere to go but ALL-IN!

Leadership Code Challenge:

Do you operate with contingency plans? Do you find that they spread your efforts, time, and energy so thin that you are not able to focus in one arena? Write down your top dreams and goals. Develop a singular plan that will put you on the right track to fully commit to one thing.

_____

_____

_____

_____

_____

_____

_____

_____

_____

_____

_____

_____

_____

_____

_____

_____

_____

_____

_____

"Growth demands a temporary surrender of security."

Gail Sheedy

Chapter 9

Grustle: Grind vs. Hustle

You hear people say "rise and grind" all the time. I'm not here to talk about those who simply use it as a catchphrase or for some hot shot hashtag, I am talking real hustle and real grind. The essence of this concept is the inspiration behind this book. Reading this chapter, you'll understand what it truly takes to not only become a leader, but also stay great as a leader. In this chapter, you will learn how I differentiate between the two, and how when you combine them, it is a powerful strategy that any leader can implement.

Let's begin with the meaning of grind. My perspective on grinding is when you're initially starting up and building a strong worth ethic. Grinding helps you possess the skillset required to level up, simply by overcompensating with hard work. A grind's foundation is built on its blood, sweat and tears. *By being proactive and participating to grow into your dreams, you have to consistently participate in the hard work necessary.* It's earned, not given. It's starting from the bottom, and stems from an urgency to succeed and gain some of life's most appealing rewards. It's special starting at the bottom, because it gives you the intangible gifts to *create remarkable skills* and *develop your character.*

You may not be the most talented or most gifted, but you are willing to go to work and unlock your potential! You learn different movements and those movements create progress and opportunity. You're rolling up your sleeves early and staying out late burning the midnight oil. Grinding takes initiative before you begin to gain long-term appreciation. Nothing beats the initiation of hard work. It's those hours of grit and grind that help you develop and master your craft.

Grinding is *on you*, there is no network, there's no resource to pull from, there's no team, it's direct effort. You grind because you want to become technically and tactically proficient. When you grind, *you learn to do so much, with so little, for so long, that you virtually can do absolutely anything with absolutely nothing.* The work ethic becomes embedded in you. It becomes engraved in your DNA and ultimately acquired for life.

Now let's talk about hustle. After you acquire the will to work hard, it's the next step. It's the hunger and the drive to do whatever it takes while you grind. Hustle is when you have a higher skillset, which either came naturally, or you obtained through the grind and experience. You have the craft, you have the intuition, and it's now about what you do with it. It's calculated; you have the network, you have the team, and there's value instilled. You're still working and pushing hard, but you've mastered work ethic and gained a lot of skills that people now notice. When you're out there hustling, you can approach situations with more confidence. **The more confidence you have**, *the more competence you gain, in everything that you do.*

When you hustle, you know you have the skills to succeed. When you're grinding, you know you can gain those skills, but you must work hard at it. *The day you graduate and apply both together, this is where you obtain the highest paradigm of your leadership* for both you and your team. If you're a great grinder, your skills are going to strengthen, and you aren't afraid to lead by example with hard work. If you're a great hustler, your effectiveness is going to get that much better and you become very efficient. The great leaders start with the grind in their work and the hustle in their heart. The only thing left for them to do is execute!

Take a look at great football players like Antonio Brown, JJ Watt and Tom Brady -- they weren't afraid of the grind. Of course, they had the great skills but they grinded and applied massive work ethic to raise their skillset to an even higher level. We are talking six round picks and a walk-on college player who are first ballot hall of famers. Antonio Brown is still training with the rookies who are hungry. Some people won't practice unless they're with the big dogs, but Antonio Brown is willing to go to work with any superstar or up-and-coming superstar as long as they are going to give it everything they've got. The world celebrates the end results of Sunday touchdowns and championship rings. I encourage you to also celebrate the person who never gave up, never gave in, and went against all the odds with perseverance and heart. This displays a true winner with both work ethic and acquired skill set. When you apply both the grind and the hustle, this is how you get into that Hall of Fame in your field.

Leaders who apply both become peak performers in everything they do. I refer to those who hit the grind and hustle as Grustlers; when you hit them both, you are applying The Grustle. These are fresh concepts here -- **grind before glory, heart before hustle**. It's a heck of a phrase but an even better concept to apply.

In order to duplicate and develop elite performers, you must have the proper "show and tell" technique. Most leaders are great at creating followers, but the true measurement of a leader is how many leaders they have developed. Leaders who fail to develop others have the problem of telling their people what to do, instead of showing them how to do it. Even worse, they will tell them what to do but never why it is important. Now on the flip side, leaders who are great at developing others are also great at breaking down the what, how, and why of every method.

You have to show them what they need to do and how they are going to do it. You must demonstrate properly and have them listen and repeat. Most importantly though, you must explain to your people why this is important. Learn how to teach the proper technique of work ethic and gained skill set and watch your team grow overnight.

I've always been a fan of boxing and I'll be the first to say that Mike Tyson was on his grind in those championship years. He was a phenomenal athlete who applied work ethic and the right mentality as he quickly climbed the ranks of boxing. Once he became the champion and the money started rolling in, he got away from what made him great.

Tyson used to say that once he became the champion, he wasn't going to train as hard anymore. Previously, he was doing high intensity training before a fight, and then just stopped doing what made him great. Once Tyson got knocked out, he understood that he needed to put in the hard work if he was going to maintain his title.

People who stop applying work ethic eventually lose their way. Mike Tyson realized that by coasting, it would never lead to his lasting success. Just as Mike Tyson learned from his mistake, you must do the same in order to achieve the success you desire.

When I switched careers, I had to trigger my mind to go back to the grind. I had the skills, confidence, and had years of experience. All of the sudden, after years of being on top of one field, I had to go back to the grind -- it was reverse engineering. I was now in a new industry where I didn't have the skills, wisdom and experience to settle like I was at the top. It required maximum grind or be a long term "has been." A lot of people get good at their job, become comfortable, and the grind goes away. If you are forced to switch careers or have to start over, that grind needs to come back. ***When it comes to hustle and grind, you need to have one just as much as the other. Good things come to those who grind. Great things come to those who hustle. The greatest things come to those who GRUSTLE.***

The Grustle is about working harder and smarter in your field and even more in leadership. Both are required to be a high-performing leader who continues to grow. You can have all the degrees in the world, but if you don't have a hustler's mentality and the ambition to grind, all will be lost. When you commit to applying the GRUSTLE mentality, you will find true success as a leader who people will want to follow. This is the true leadership code.

Leadership Code Challenge:

Give an example of a time you grinded and then of a time you hustled. In what areas can you work harder? In what areas can you become more efficient? What steps can you take to combine the two so that you continue to evolve on your leadership journey?

_____

_____

_____

_____

_____

_____

_____

_____

_____

_____

_____

_____

_____

_____

_____

_____

_____

_____

"Go the extra mile, there's no one on it."

Grant Cardone

Chapter 10

Be True to Who You Are: Authentic Swag

Authenticity is the purest form of who you are. I believe it to be a gold standard in leadership. The law of attraction says that you are going to attract what you put out into the world. It is so vital to embrace individuality as well as authenticity, and there is no real win any other way. Problems can arise when you are putting on a front as a leader because you can potentially attract the wrong people.

This happens because you're not acting like yourself. You're trying to act like someone or something else that you assume you should be, but I'm here to tell you, authenticity is a different game. You are not born or built to model everyone else, especially as a leader. *Don't get caught up in following the masses, you'll eventually realize the "m" is silent.* Authentic leaders never settle, always give off authentic vibes, find authentic solutions, and are always surrounded by authentic people.

Authenticity is when love and truth come *before* what others think of you. It is when you truly are who you are, and your actions are congruent with your personality. This type of authenticity encourages trust, confidence and loyalty. When being true, the wrong people in your life are going to leave you and the right people are going to stay.

I understand the concept of "fake it 'til you make it," but you can't fake who you are. ***If you're authentic with your imperfections, people will gravitate towards you***. If you're battle-tested and have walked through fiery circumstances, people are going to want to follow that tenacity and fire. Authenticity will draw people into you. They will be willing to fight for what they want, and they will be willing to fight for you. They will follow you wherever you are going. That is true authentic swag.

The best leaders have an authentic and genuine character. These leaders are not free from flaws, in fact, they have accepted their imperfections and are okay with being vulnerable. All the while, staying honest, flexible, and are continuously learning from those flaws. Flexibility doesn't mean that they're changing who they are, instead it means that they roll with the punches and amend their strategies when necessary. Authentic leaders are not changing their character, their morals, or their ethics. That's where people can get mixed up. They fall into the trap of getting caught up in the money, and they can easily lose sight of who they are as a result.

I admire several leaders, some of whom I've worked with, and others from a distance. Whether through audio books, podcasts, or social media, authentic character shines through. Tony Robbins, Ed Mylett, Gerard Adams, and Andy Frisella stand out to me as elite leaders -- they are all badass in their own way. They are long-distance mentors to me. I appreciate that Robbins has next-level knowledge and psychological education to better people.

Frisella is brutally honest with full intentions of keeping it real and factual to help people. Adams is creative and an influential leader who focuses on bettering today's millennials. Mylett instills passion with powerful tutelage to contribute and impact people for the better.

Each of these leaders are genuine to who they are and serve a purpose to influence others daily. All of the above names have abundance mentalities, big hearts, are extremely humble, and stay authentic to who they are to create a better world.

Authentic leaders always prove to be self-aware and genuine; they know when they are in an environment that doesn't feel right. If that happens to you, *always trust your gut and instinct*, it will always steer you in the right direction. Trust your roots, your upbringing, and what you know to be right -- it's already inside you.

The way you see yourself matters far more than the way others see you. You're an original. You come as a valuable, authentic version. No one wants to buy a fake Louis Vuitton, they want the real thing. Know that if you come in as a carbon copy, trying to be someone or something that you aren't, nobody is going to buy it. They want someone to be an authentic leader, not a phony.

As they say, **"you have to stand for something or you're going to fall for anything."** When it comes to authenticity as a concept in its realest form, it's a matter of *who you are*. If you're trying to be someone you're not, there's nothing magnetic about it and most won't be willing to follow.

Albert Mehrabian is a psychology professor who studied both verbal and non-verbal communication. The statistical results of his studies ruled that communication is only 7% verbal and 93% non-verbal. The non-verbal component was made up of body language (55%) and tone of voice (38%). If you are not authentic, your people will subconsciously pick it up.

The truest leader is 100% authentic and plays to their style and to their brand. You cannot lose when you're playing to your brand. With that being said, it's okay if you don't fully know and understand who you are yet. As both people and leaders, we are constantly growing and evolving into better versions of ourselves. It's important to stay authentic and real when elevating. In whatever phase you are in, there's more power in keeping it real than you could ever imagine.

Authentic swag is all about being who you are, holding to your ideals and values, celebrating your successes, owning your failures, and being the best *you* that you can be. You are your best investment, your best gift, and the people who desire to follow you deserve no less than your authentic self.

Leadership Code Challenge:

Name some mentors that you appreciate. What authentic qualities do they demonstrate? Have you ever tried to be someone you aren't? Have you found success in your own authentic swag? Make a list of truths about you that you are willing to own and advance with, capitalizing on who you are.

_____

_____

_____

_____

_____

_____

_____

_____

_____

_____

_____

_____

_____

_____

_____

_____

_____

"I had no idea that being your authentic self could make me as rich as I've become. If I had, I'd have done it a lot earlier."

Oprah Winfrey

Chapter 11

Goal Diggin'—Lead by Design Not By Default

Goals are crucial if you are going to lead by design. In order to accomplish what you set out to do, goals are necessary to establish *progress* and *clarity* when aiming for and hitting your targets. Everyone is so focused on social media and what everyone else is doing that they forget to focus and take the time to set aside time for their very own goals. A lot of leaders have an excellent hustle and a top-notch grind, but their goal setting habits are not in place. It is important to get in the habit of quality goal setting. ***First you create the habits, and then the habits create you.***

A secret of the best leaders is that they have established and mastered a daily routine of writing their goals down. I can't emphasize this enough. You can live your life in a way that is built by *design*, or in a way that is built by *default*. You decide -- which one do you think will bring greater leadership success?

The fact of the matter is that when you do not write any of your goals down, you are just falling into default. You float through the day-to-day with a diminished focus and a lack of purpose. Plan ahead, set goals, stick to them, and watch your life transform.

Goals don't have to just be within the realm of business. There is no need to limit your potential. There is a science behind the act of writing down goals and the positive impacts they can hold in all aspects of your life. You can write down family goals, personal growth goals, social goals, public service goals, or even fitness goals. These goals are like enormous magnets. The bigger, more compelling, and purposeful they are, the stronger the pull will be to obtain the results.

I not only write down my goals, but I also activate alarms in my phone, especially if my schedule is full, otherwise I'd forget. Establishing and writing down goals helps you to be efficient with both *time* and *productivity*.

Here's the breakdown, and this is fact: **when people write down their goals, they're 42% more likely to get**

them to come to fruition simply by just writing them down on a regular basis. There is a science behind that, and here's why.

The right side of the brain is the creativity side. Your goal begins as an idea, but when you write it down, it goes into the left side of your brain which is the logical side of your brain. At this point, logic meets creativity, creativity meets logic. When these two meet up and combine, you're subconsciously creating logic and you then *start to make things happen.*

In order for our goals to come to life, we must intentionally apply action. *Remember that an inch of execution reaches much further than a mile of theory.* My leadership team sets monthly goals the first week of every month. They are completely congruent with our monthly and end-of-the-year goals. We never try to lower the goal, and if we miss it, we make up for it in other areas. Some people make the common error of lowering the goal. Instead, you may just have to compensate in other areas or find other areas to make up ground.

It is important to recognize and award everyone when team goals are hit. We make it a point to find time to bond and celebrate as a team. It could be Top Golf, a party at Dave and Busters, sporting events, or even picnics. It's beneficial to incentivize team goals, bring everyone together, and equally as important to not overlook a job well-done.

Knowing all of this, I want to ask you a question. Who is more likely to accomplish their goals? The person who writes down their goals every single day or the one that does it once every two years? Which of these two leaders is being proactive and is on the disciplined track to accomplish their mission?

By writing down your goals you always have something in your ear or in your face -- it's always on your mind. You're constantly thinking of it, which forces you to logically strategize. You also don't have to limit yourself to just daily goals, there are bigger-picture options to seize. You can look a bit further out and establish weekly, monthly, annual, 3-year goals, 5-year goals, and even 10-year goals

No matter what, your goals need to be realistic and purpose-driven with a compounding effect to get you what you want. These goals have to be specific, so figure out what you want and where you want to be. From there, it is crucial that you set deadlines and have urgency for each and every goal. Yet again, keep in mind you won't be praised or rewarded for preparing your goals, but in time, you will be praised publicly when those goals come to fruition.

Being prepared is your best weapon against lacking confidence, anxiety, and uncertainty. You never know how close you are to the gold when working towards your goals. Don't confuse gold with gold-plated, though. Those who are gold-plated never wrote down their goals. Don't be gold-plated, be gold!

My favorite formula for establishing goals is by using the **S.M.A.R.T. Goals** system.

Your goals should be:

> **S** - Specific;
> **M** - Measurable;
> **A** - Attainable;
> **R** - Relevant/rewarding;
> **T** - Timebound/Trackable.

Anytime you need to get people to set goals, you go back to this simplistic formula. Understanding the importance of the structure, you can actually track progress because you don't just have the goal, you have the *details*.

Today's society will match their ties, their shirts, they'll even match their purses with their shoes, **but they won't match their goals with their actions**. Maybe that's why Bill Gates and Mark Zuckerberg never wear ties, they're focused on matching their goals with their actions. Maybe, maybe not? Either way, they make sure those goals are congruent with the direction and action they take.

It is crucial to establish growth goals, because you always need to have goals to grow. Ask, "What book are you going to read this month?," "When do I want to promote people?," "How quickly until I scale my business?," "What areas am I going to work on developing the team?" or "What are this month's growth and production goals?" Be sure to manage your goals with data and motivate your team goals with emotion.

I don't plan out everything in life, like when I'm hanging out with my family it's a bit more relaxed. But there have to be goals. When are you going to have family time? When will you have gym time? When are you going to shut it down and put your phone on airplane mode, etc.?

Goal setting is your master plan to success. Establish your goals, invest time into the game plan, and follow through with immediate action.

Know that you have the skills, knowledge and willpower to be the greatest of leaders. While goal digging, don't allow your lack of discipline to prevent you from reaching your highest level. I challenge you to make your life a masterpiece by your designed goals. This will help you join the ranks of the elite leaders. Accept the challenge of goal setting to motivate and guide you to a successful outcome!

Leadership Code Challenge:

Get in the habit of writing down at least one daily goal for yourself. What are your upcoming week goals? What are your monthly goals? What are your annual goals? Set realistic targets that are obtainable and follow through with measurable action.

_____

_____

_____

_____

_____

_____

_____

_____

_____

_____

_____

_____

_____

_____

_____

"People with goals succeed because they know where they are going."

Earl Nightingale

Chapter 12

Get R.I.C.H. -- Realize I Create Happiness

One of the best things a leader can do is realize *how* to create happiness. I have learned that you have to put *happiness* and *energy* into what you do, and that it starts from the top. I frequently say that **positive vibes are the newest currency**. We want to go places where we enjoy life because we aren't supposed to be miserable, but in so many work environments, many of us are.

Studies have shown that on Friday and Sunday nights these unhappy people are looking for new jobs. They dread Monday and do not want to go back to what they consider a "miserable job." What an unfortunate use of a weekend! All it takes to turn around the environment and culture of these miserable workplaces is the influence of a positive leader.

Energy and positive vibes are the secret homemade sauce for a leader. It's an inside job -- all the positivity and happiness in the work life stems from the leaders, then to the people, and then to the clients. It goes from the top down and it is your responsibility to initiate as a leader.

Everybody knows that Google, Nike, American Income, and Apple have unbelievable culture. It's no surprise they are all powerhouse corporations because they all make sure that their company runs on positive vibes. It's their thing, it's their reputation, and it starts with their leadership.

Unfortunately, a lot of leaders aren't fluent with positivity and good vibes, and with this concept, you definitely have to find ways to go the extra mile. In order to get **R.I.C.H.,** remember **"Realize.I.Create.Happiness."** It is your fiduciary duty as a leader to create the vibe.

A key to maintaining positivity is that you can never bring in your problems or use social media to vent your frustrations. Great leaders don't ***Facebook their problem, they face their problem.*** You can't put your issues on other people because that is extra weight that they now have to carry. Be cautious about who you share your burdens with. Never complain or be negative towards the people who follow you because nobody wants to follow that type of leader. Rather, learn how to press pause and come up with a logical, non-emotional solution. Don't be the leader who has problems, be the leader who provides solutions to everyone's problems.

Too often, leaders will get caught up in money, quotas, or growth, all which are important, BUT the bottom line is that numbers are *infinite*. If you are only chasing numbers for happiness, you'll be chasing infinity. By the time you hit a number, you're simply chasing a new number. Everyone knows it's impossible to catch infinity, you'll be chasing it forever, causing you to never find fulfillment. Without fulfillment, you'll never be truly happy, because it will never be enough. You'll never be building on the reserves of what you do have, but rather always be chasing what you don't have.

The richest leaders are rich in knowledge, servanthood, happiness, life, love, and are surrounded by great people. Being a positive leader doesn't mean that you're waking up happy or are the most positive person every single day. Instead, it's learning to wake up and find the most positive outcomes in the challenges that come. **Positive thought has to be intentional.** You should start every waking day with a positive thought. One positive affirmation to start your day can change the entire day. This sounds easy and obvious but common sense needs to become common practice for you as a leader.

My agency exhibits an incredibly positive culture because culture cultivates the atmosphere. We asked our people what makes them tick besides money and they replied, "Recognition and appreciation." As a leader, you may have to consistently recognize your people for a job well done. Lack of recognition leads to a lack of motivation and happiness which can deflate the culture you work hard to create. Always remember to show constant love and appreciation towards your people.

Do not get consumed by the day-to-day responsibilities that distance yourself from the team. Keep them close and keep it real. Your role as their leader is to hold standards to a high level but keep culture fun at the same time.

Through trial and error, we have learned that an enjoyable environment leads to results, so we keep everything light and fun. Just because we're making money and doing incredible work, doesn't mean we can't be fun and foster passion, growth, and teamwork.

There's a lot of uniqueness to making people happy, it isn't a cookie-cutter thing. Each person on your team is unique, and when you're working as a leader, you have to figure out every individual need to motivate or incentivize.

What is their "why"? Is it millions of dollars or a lifestyle that promotes freedom? What do they need? Is it *growth, certainty, significance* or *love and connection*? It is important to find what fuels them. If you don't have a relationship, you don't know what influences them. You want to always build relationships and eliminate ego when building bonds with the team.

I have a great story that was passed along to me by a mentor about happiness.

> *"A man tells Buddha "I want happiness."*
> *Buddha replies: "Remove "I," that's ego.*
> *Then remove "want," that's desire.*
> *Now you are left with happiness!"*

It's a *simple* story with humor, but also a very relevant point when creating happiness for yourself and for your teammates. You have to be smart as a leader. You have to show them you care, know what drives them, and create a unified culture for all.

Money doesn't motivate everyone. Some people want more family time, growth, connection, awards, achievement – these are the things that make people perform better. That's why you have to build genuine relationships with your people so that you can exude your most effective influence.

Grant Cardone has a concept of a "No negativity zone" and we follow in suit to create that spirit. Remember how to get R.I.C.H. -- Realize I Create Happiness. Remember and apply these words because your team's happiness is a direct reflection of their leader's ability to lead.

Leadership Code Challenge:

Consider what motivates and incentivizes you. What makes you happy? What makes the people you lead happy? Based on the ideas in this chapter, develop a list of at least five incentives that you can consider bringing to your people -- remember to make them varied and unique.

_____

_____

_____

_____

_____

_____

_____

_____

_____

_____

_____

_____

_____

_____

_____

_____

_____

_____

"A person who is happy is not because everything is right in his life. He is happy because his attitude towards everything in his life is right."

Sundar Pichai

Chapter 13

S.C.A.M. Your People

How many times have you heard people say, "If it's too good to be true, it must be a scam"? Or when *you* become successful, they assume that you achieved your level of success by scamming others? Clearly you MUST be scamming if you are successful and it appears too good to be true. Right? Wrong.

Unless you S.C.A.M. your people on my terms… then they might be right, but it isn't what you think! I coined a new term that *insists* you S.C.A.M. your people! That's right scam them as much as possible. In leadership, the key combinations behind this acronym consider relationships, influence, and true servanthood.

It's about less self, more serve. Before I break that down, I want to go into a story about a time I failed to S.C.A.M. someone close to me, and in doing so, I also failed myself.

I never can remember things that I do for people, I just do them. I'm not keeping score, but I'll tell you what I do remember -- I remember the opportunities that I missed to step up and do the right thing. One missed opportunity can easily outweigh one hundred seized opportunities.

When I was on my early hustle and grind, I sacrificed my free time, social relationships and time with my family. It was easy to lose that balance because I was constantly pushing my efforts to prove myself. This is not uncommon when you have that overpowering sense of urgency as a leader.

You will miss birthdays, dinners, and events when committing to hard work and dedication, but you cannot miss opportunities to empower teammates. During this time, one of my best performers and now great friends had a standout month. She was such an elite performer whose results were always expected, and when you start to expect, you can easily overlook appreciation and gratitude. We had a record-breaking month and she had a record-breaking performance.

Due to the non-stop schedule, I had completely overlooked how much she had done. I let her down, and weeks later when she let me know about it, I never felt so small. I learned a lot about myself at that early stage in my career because I observed and reflected on my own actions instead of another's. Moving forward, our relationship became stronger and that mistake never happened again. Empowering people as a leader has to become a strength because it fills them with energy and fulfilment.

At the time, I was not being the person I was born to be. I was expected to celebrate and recognize this standout who now is a lifelong friend. I now know the value of hitting pause, realigning, and never taking things for granted.

This is just one example of the importance of caring for others and sacrificing self when the time comes. Through this story and my work experience, I have developed this guide to become a caring, connected leader.

I encourage you to also S.C.A.M. your people.
Sacrifice. Celebrate. Appreciate. Mentor.

S stands for **Sacrifice**. This relates to giving back to your people regularly without expecting to receive and doing things unannounced. Leadership isn't a punch-in/punch-out position, it's a privilege. When you sacrifice for your team, it gains loyalty, which again is a privilege. The people I have the opportunity to lead do things because they care, not because they have to. You cannot get this twisted as a leader because the moment you do, you are in trouble. So what are you willing to sacrifice? (Please do note that you're a leader and not a savior, that sacrifice goes both ways, and I won't pour all my time into someone who couldn't care less about the vision).

    C represents **Celebrating your people**. There's a lot of joy, loyalty and recognition in celebrating daily progress. You must sincerely believe in your people, have authentic celebration, and highlight all their achievements. Authentic celebration helps your team grow confidence, improve their skills, strengthen their craft, and will shine that spotlight on their potential and drive. In team sports, it's always important to celebrate together. Remember if it was big to you during your come up, it's big to them now. Whether they expect it or not, as a leader you have to find both big and small wins to celebrate.

    A is all about **Appreciating your people**. Magnify their strengths and always display great appreciation. Be grateful, never hateful toward your people whether they're getting the results or not. You cannot afford to be a bipolar leader! These people are putting their lives in your hands for good reason. You may have to press pause and realize that, just as I realized from my story above. Gratitude daily, plus love daily, equals quality appreciation.

And lastly, **M is for Mentorship**. There's no blueprint more successful than hard work and productivity. Every leader was a great follower before they were a great leader. You had mentors give to you and now it's your time to help give back and develop a road map to help them along the way. You have to commit to add value to your people regularly. In truth, they want a leader and a navigator. Do you set time aside to work with and develop your team? Do you map out their individual goals?

Unfortunately, my S.C.A.M. method isn't the workplace normality, which is why people are looking for new places to work. Their house doesn't feel like a home because they don't feel important. People are always jumping ship because they are just there for the paycheck, not for the big picture. Without a strong leader, there is no emotional attachment.

By applying this concept regularly, it shows you take no one for granted and by doing so, retain loyalty. When you don't have something, you place a high value on it. When you have it, you don't always appreciate it. When you lose it, because you didn't do all of these things, it goes right back up in value to you. As they say, "You don't know what you've got 'til it's gone." So why lose valuable people due to a lack of valuable leadership?

I wasn't fortunate to always be in a leadership role though. I jumped straight from college into the steel business and didn't have people to S.C.A.M. because I didn't have a team or anyone to lead early in my career. Now, I have a team and am able to build on that foundation. You have to be proactive with "scamming" the right people.

Your people are more likely to stay on board with a company because of unity. You build influence and forge genuine relationships when you put *their* needs before *your* needs. **You want to be the type of leader who walks into the room and says, *"There you are!"* instead of *"Here I am!"*** Learn how to S.C.A.M. your people the right way and watch not only how they grow in a positive light, but also how you ultimately grow as a leader.

Leadership Code Challenge:

Can you think of times in your past jobs where you felt truly appreciated and celebrated? How did that make you feel? What actions were taken to keep you feeling as though you were part of a team? How can you, as a leader, bring the S.C.A.M. method to your own team?

_____

_____

_____

_____

_____

_____

_____

_____

_____

_____

_____

_____

_____

_____

_____

_____

_____

_____

_____

"Real success is not defined by what you accomplish. It is defined by how you are helping others accomplish."

Andy Frisella

Chapter 14

Unification of a Team

Just because you have a group of people, it doesn't automatically make them a team. The most effective leaders depend on their ability to fully *connect* and *inspire* their people without relying on their position. Great leaders unify their team and understand that they have to apply big goals, big dreams and happiness. Unification identifies a true team.

Let's look at basketball, specifically the 1992 USA Men's Olympic team. The team proved to be unbeatable. You had players like Larry Bird, Michael Jordan, Magic Johnson, Charles Barkley, and Patrick Ewing, just to name a few. These Hall of Famers unified the three major ingredients by having a **common goal**, **connecting**, and **collaborating**, thus creating what was known as *The Dream Team*. They never lost because they brought their talents together and unified as one.

Conversely, I can think back to my childhood days of playing sports. There were those coaches we all had that always played their own kid, again and again, no matter how weak the kid's skill set may have been. The entire time, the rest of the team questioned why this same kid was on the field over and over again. Eventually the team became frustrated and disinterested. This is an example of ineffective leadership. There was no common goal, there was no playing to strength, and there was no thinking of the team as a whole. There was no unification.

It's amazing how you play better when you have both confidence and your team to back you up. Teams with common goals, in sports and business, win big with great team spirit. **Common goals** encourage complete buy-in. Without them, you easily stunt the destination, and almost always fall short. Every great team knows the line, *"If you want to run fast, run alone; if you want to run far, run together."*

I have always instilled the dream team mentality into my players. Last year, we were going for gold in our agency but were far behind, heading into the last quarter of the year. We had major ground to make up, which to most, would have been impossible to achieve. The odds were stacked against us and we knew we would ultimately fall short if we didn't formulate a game plan. We came together as a leadership team and had incredible buy-in from everyone, and most importantly, connected to a common goal to win together. There was a tremendous amount of sacrifice from this group of individuals.

Slowly we were starting to catch up, however we knew that it would take everything we had up to the last week of the year to win. The team became obsessed with supporting and encouraging one another to the finish. The last day of the year finally arose and our collective efforts ceased the victory, by a very small margin.

This win would have never been possible without the dedication of the team, belief instilled by leadership and a connection to common goal. True championship teams are built not by the display of their skills, but by working together to accomplish the mission.

The common goal of your team has to be one and the same. Oftentimes people enter a company because the job meets income standards, yet there is a major disconnect because they don't know about the company, its mission, or its vision. If you're just individually chasing a paycheck, you aren't going to have the value that the team needs. This is where the leader steps in to connect and unify the individual with the big picture.

Dream Team Leaders are not self-made. The power of the team comes from how committed they are to one another, and from how unified they are with the common goal. How does a leader approach the task of unifying a team? Obviously it's more than just a common goal, right?

Although communication is vital, I say that the #1 thing you can do is **connect** with your people. You can learn a lot from watching and listening to them. Make it a point to listen to *understand*, not just listen to *respond*. Listen to exactly what they're saying to you and answer accordingly.

Remember to use your authentic swag when connecting with your people. Give sincere compliments and even ask for their feedback

An ego-driven leader hears feedback as criticism. This type of leadership isn't for the confident, authentic individual such as yourself. It is also very important that when asking for feedback you learn from it and not get defensive. Listen to adjust, to properly pivot, to understand, and to be open-minded. Listen in a genuine way that is free from judgment, and it will build trust and connection with your people. *Leaders who never let people be heard are eventually surrounded by a team that no longer has anything to say.*

I always look for ways to proactively form some type of commonality with people to bring down any defensive walls they may have. It is important to relate and even more important to show vulnerability.

If your story is always picture-perfect, it's hard to connect, it isn't believable, and makes it difficult to find common ground. **As a leader, it is important to find common ground, so you can take them to higher ground.** You may not act like them or have the same habits or hobbies, but there is always commonality to connect. It's important to consistently make efforts to demonstrate that you mean what you say.

To communicate to my team that I am genuine, I always use their names or even nicknames, and always make sure I add the personal touch. You must talk about the things they enjoy talking about. You don't always have to ask about numbers and quotas. If the conversation always revolves around the business, then it's not personal and you're not bridging a connection. As a leader, remember real connections are built on giving more than you take.

Be aware some people aren't interested in connecting. They are closed-minded and are hard to coach. Understand that the ones who are not making the connection are the ones who are going to have difficulty succeeding in a team setting. Don't beat yourself up over it. You aren't going to win every single game and win over every single person.

The third component to a unified team is to **collaborate** with your people -- plan for something bigger than yourself. The major key to success, and it's almost a lost art, is *collaboration*. Most people are only one *collaboration* away from changing their lives.

In the game "Red Rover," you're only as strong as your weakest link. It's important to collaborate in a position of strength when locking arms. You, as a leader, will become the weakest if you disconnect from your people because you believe you are above them. If a leader is not performing, they may disconnect from the team because of embarrassment. If the leader is achieving superior results, they may tend to put themselves above the team because they are on their high horse. Neither are the best approach in unifying. The best way to overcome and strengthen is by *collaborating*. It is one of the most vital ingredients to creating a dream team.

An effective leader understands that when unifying, it is crucial to be helpful, collaborative, and to participate in the give and take. A true leader doesn't just bark orders, this power player works *with* the team.

As stated earlier, a unified team needs a **common goal, connection,** and **collaboration**. Focus on something that is inspirational over motivational. Typical motivation refers to motive. Often the *motive* is materialistic, like jewelry, a house, or a car. When referring to inspiration, that is something that runs much deeper. The word *inspire stems from "in spirit,"* and this is where the foundation lies within your team. When your team is inspired, they are ready to walk through flames to win any great victory, no matter what it may be. When your team is on the same page of the big picture with *collective goals, connection, collaboration,* and are inspired, they will make massive power moves together.

When leading a team, the goal is to humanize yourself as much as possible. Connect with them, find ways to collaborate, and inspire them with common goals-- that's how the strong leaders cultivate a team into ONE.

Leadership Code Challenge:

Would you define yourself as a team player? Do you connect with your team? If not, what ways can you start connecting? Does everyone believe in the common goals? If not, where can we improve?

Are you willing to put in the extra time and effort necessary to collaborate more often and more effectively with your team?

_____

_____

_____

_____

_____

_____

_____

_____

_____

_____

_____

_____

_____

_____

_____

_____

"Talent wins games, but teamwork and intelligence wins championships."

Michael Jordan

Chapter 15

Mindset: Learn to Be Mentally Tough

We've all heard the expression, "A penny for your thoughts?" I want to ask, are your thoughts even worth a penny?

The absolute best leaders have unbreakable mindsets. These leaders are super confident, and their mind is a beautiful thing once channeled properly. Let's look at the lion, known as the king of the jungle. The lion isn't the biggest, the strongest, the heaviest, and he isn't the fastest. What the lion possesses and embodies is extreme confidence, and because of that, he commands great respect.

In order to position yourself as the leader you desire to become, *your thoughts have to match those of the person you want to become.*

All leaders take responsibility to be mentally tough. **Leaders who are unstoppable from the neck up are unstoppable from the neck down.** You must be mentally tough before you become physically tough in any arena.

When you're talking about mental toughness, ask yourself "Are you going to have a *worrier* mentality or a *warrior mentality*?" Warriors are fearless, free from doubt, and their mental state is to fight until they succeed. On the other side of the coin, the worriers accept defeat, play the blame game, focus on external circumstances, are prisoners of their past, and ask, "Why me?" rather than "Try me!"

The worrying mind simply kills one's dreams. Why such anxiety? Many will worry about their past, about money, about other people, about the right timing. I'll say this right here and right now: **It's never going to be the right time**! There is no perfect setting. You create that perfect time. It's the warriors who fight until they succeed. They have their immense confidence and lack of doubt that create the **"right time."** So again, are you going to mentally be a *warrior* or a *worrier* in your leadership mission?

I remember one time when my back was against the wall. I was losing friends, teammates, and was in the hardest place mentally I have ever been -- a true breaking point. It's funny how life's adversities have many ways of testing our *will*. Sometimes it's like nothing is happening at all, and other times it's like everything is happening all at once. You know how they say that when it rains it pours? I had accepted that. I also accepted that if I wanted it to stop pouring, it was time to make an adjustment. Mentally, it becomes less about adversity, and more about asking yourself: Do you want it bad enough? Can you run this race? Can you do it the right way? Can you not cut corners? And when the shit hits the fan, how do you handle it?

In Tim S. Grover's book *Relentless: From Good to Great to Unstoppable*, he highlights his opinion of mental toughness between sports legends Charles Barkley and Tiger Woods. He retells the story of how Barkley got into an altercation with a man at a bar who was instigating him. When asked if he would do anything different, Barkley responded with no apologies or remorse, and took full ownership of the situation, with zero regret. In Grover's mind, this ownership demonstrates familiarity with adversity and high levels of mental toughness.

Woods doesn't get such a glowing review though. Woods, who got caught stepping out on his wife, didn't know how to handle it because he never experienced adversity at this level. Tiger was an iconic superstar with no flaws throughout life. He didn't confront it head on, and mentally it lingered, taking him way off of his golf game. Adversity hit him all at once. A decade later, Woods is just now becoming competitive.

So what's the moral of Grover's story? Welcome mental toughness and adversity into your life, so that when something happens, you don't suffer a major crash.

The hard truth is that it won't be easy and that you have got to have the mental capacity to handle the setbacks of life. Everyone reacts differently to these adversities. However you choose to view them, either good or bad, recognize you have made it through them all. How you look at challenges is very important. Ask, *is it happening TO me or is it happening FOR me?* What is your perspective?

Some people, when they experience pain, are afraid of it and get stuck in the pain. From there, that pain continues and develops into non-stop suffering. The difference between the *warrior* mind and the *worrier* mind shines through here. A warrior knows that pain will be replaced by growth or even something better. Because of the pain, they are only getting closer to where they want to be. Never give up when going through pain because if you give up, the regret will be far more painful than anything else you have ever felt. For a great leader like yourself, it is always too soon to quit.

Henry Ford famously stated, **"Whether you believe you can, or believe you can't, you're right."** Your thoughts as a leader are silently rewarded when your team plays above the standard. However, when things are not going your way, you must have the mental toughness to self-evaluate, self-reflect, and create a game plan for your team to get to the next level. When you fixate your thoughts on winning, you find a way to make it happen.

Believe it or not, we think about the same thoughts every day. 91% are fixed and only 9% of our thoughts are variable. That is the margin between those who say, "I can" and those who say, "I can't." It seems like a small measure, but it makes all the difference when becoming mentally unstoppable.

Most people have the similar life goal of obtaining the right methods in their business while earning a lot of money, but do not know how to get started. It all starts with the right mentality and mental toughness. When you are in the right mental state and have mental toughness, it will put you on the right track of creating a successful future. If your *mindset* is right, then your *methods* will follow. This allows you to be able to scale your business on good practices, and in turn, the money will flow abundantly.

Individuals mess this up when they focus on the money first. Their ethics crumble and they get shaky on the business practices. They think, "We can bend this," or "We can cut corners here." These people only have one thing in mind -- the money. Which leads to large problems quickly. *The leader who always chooses money over people will eventually have neither.*

If your priorities are out of order, you are no longer mentally tough enough to realize that you are doing what is easy, not what is right. When I think about making a decision, I go back to my roots, and mentally hear my grandmother's voice echoing to *"do the right thing."*

This is blunt, but if the mindset is not there, you shouldn't even run the race. If your mind is not conditioned properly, the second something goes wrong, you're going to break your stride which will in turn, break you.

Great leaders have clear vision and constantly see themselves where they want to be in the future. There will be times in your life where worrisome situations come up, but understand that you have power, because you make your choices. It all starts with the right mindset, choices, and your belief system.

Manifestation starts with our thoughts and is rewarded by our choices. If you manage your thoughts and actions, then your dreams, visions, and feelings will manifest into the reality you choose. It's constantly a work in progress.

When you're going for that rare air, the air will get thin. You need to live in the future and mentally believe wholeheartedly that you're going to be there. Block out the noise and have that mental tunnel vision. You may subconsciously beat yourself up, but know that this is you vs. you, and you can and will win the fight.

It is important that you constantly say positive affirmations to yourself. I encourage doing them right when you wake up. Even if you silently think words of positivity, your subconscious mind can hear it. Of all the people on the planet, you talk to yourself more than anyone. Be sure you are always saying the right things. You can subconsciously strengthen your mind on a whole new level by applying positive affirmation and mental pictures. Just because *we* can't look into our future with our physical eyes, it doesn't mean that *you* can't do this mentally. Positive thoughts lead to positive words, which lead to positive actions with positive results.

As a great leader, you need to believe in yourself and you need to project that belief so that others will believe in you. I fully believe you have to believe you can achieve anything you want. Your mental toughness can only come after all the battles you have fought and from all the times that you didn't give up. Mentally tough leaders don't waiver. Even if you have doubt, you're going to hit pause and realize, "I didn't come this far to only get this far." It's the mind that controls the body and when your mind is right, you become unstoppable. When things are getting tough, know that you're about to level up. That mindset will take you further than any talent or genetics that you have. Your mindset is everything.

Again, mentally tough people realize, "This isn't happening *to* me, it's happening *for* me, so I won't be stagnant." People think that success or leadership is just a stop. You're not supposed to stop. You don't stop. If you don't go through hardships, you won't be relatable. People can't relate to those who haven't gone through adversity. People that I admire, who I believe are truly mentally strong, have experienced adversity and have come out stronger as a result. In order to be successful, you *have* to be mentally tough. The most successful of leaders usually were the ones who could mentally withstand the most.

Tony Robbins said it best when he said, **"Your biography is not your destiny."** Where you start and where you finish is reliant upon the conscious decisions you will make along the way. You choose whether or not to tap into your roots and establish your authentic self. You choose to set goals, establish a vision, and be a reliant source of positivity and perseverance. You choose whether to grind, to hustle, or -- even better -- to Grustle. You choose to be a mentally tough warrior or a stalled-out worrier. You decide if your dreams are worth pursuing and if you're ready to run your race with blinders on. And you choose whether or not to create a legacy by drawing and providing strength, motivation, and inspiration to and from others as a leader.

It's your choice: are you ready to live by the Leadership Code?

Leadership Code Challenge:

Now that you have completed my book, it's time to make some lists: write down any of the personal development books that I mentioned that you're interested in reading; write down any quotes and acronyms that resonated with you so you can begin to apply them to your leadership journey; and start listing your goals and steps necessary to become the powerhouse leader you desire to become.

_____

_____

_____

_____

_____

_____

_____

_____

_____

_____

_____

_____

_____

"If you want to be tough mentally, it is simple:

BE TOUGHER. Don't meditate on it."

Jocko Willink

Thank you for reading my book!

I hope that this book has added value to your life.

May I ask you a quick favor? If this book has added value to your life, if you feel like you're better off after reading it, and you see that THE LEADERSHIP CODE can be a new beginning for you, I'm hoping you'll do something for someone you love:

Give this book to them. Let them borrow your copy. Ask them to read it. Or better yet, get them their own copy, maybe as a birthday or Christmas gift.

Or it could be for no special occasion at all, other than to say, "Hey, I love and appreciate you, and I want to help you live your best life. Read this." Sometimes a book is all a person needs to get back on track.

If you believe, as I do, that being a great friend or family member is about helping your friends and loved ones to become the best versions of themselves, I encourage you to share this book with them.

THE LEADERSHIP CODE is how I am able to live my dream life. It's time for others to live theirs, too.

Britton Costa

Made in the USA
Columbia, SC
08 January 2019